Elizabeth Skoglund

You Can Be YOUR OWN CHILD'S Counselor

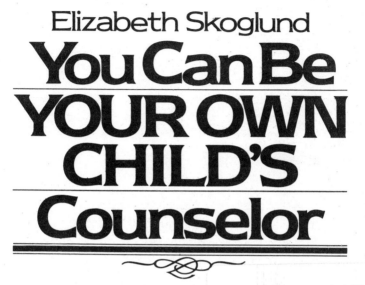

D0782640

A Division of G/L Publications
Glendale, California, U.S.A.

Other good Regal reading
Can I Talk to You? by Elizabeth Skoglund
Why Can't I Learn? by Robert D. Carpenter
Dare to Discipline by James Dobson
Too Big to Spank by Jay Kesler

Scripture quotations in this publication, unless other-
wise indicated, are from *The Living Bible*, Copyright
© 1971 by Tyndale House Publishers, Wheaton, Illinois.
Used by permission.
Other quotations are from the Authorized King James
Version *(KJV)*.

Published by Regal Books Division, G/L Publications
Glendale, California 91209
Printed in U.S.A.

Library of Congress Catalog Card No. 78-53227
ISBN 0-8307-0565-1

To Alicia Petty
For her encouragement in my writing
For her innovative ways with children
For her enthusiasm and trust

CONTENTS

FOREWORD

For about a quarter of a century now, my field of endeavor has been the surgery of children. In working with children this way, it has been necessary to manage my patients' problems in the setting of the family as would a pediatrician—observing the interaction between child and family in illness and in health. In caring for the thousands of patients that have been entrusted to me, I have, quite naturally, developed some rather strong feelings that relate to the process of giving children a fair shake. This is something that is not always done even by the most well-meaning parents.

Paradoxical though it may seem, Christian parents have more pitfalls to avoid than do parents who are not trying to raise their children in the nurture and the admonition of the Lord.

Christian parents, through family tradition or through what they believe to be divine guidance, synthesize a behavior pattern that is acceptable in their own family circle and which can stand scrutiny in the Christian community. Unfortunately, strict adherence to peripheral matters of conduct assume the same importance as usually accepted Christian prohibitions. Stealing and going to the movies on Sunday—or perhaps going to the movies at all—often become equivalent. Christianity is a dynamic religion which is based upon first knowing Christ and then loving and serving Him; it is not following a set of rules, long or short.

Another stumbling block for the Christian in child rearing is a fear of anything that might be in the realm of psychology or, even worse, in the realm of psychiatry. Some parents who believe that a state of constant good health is the right of their children and who seek pediatric medical advice at the first sniffle will shun professional psychiatric advice when their child has become unmanageable at home and a terror in the community. There is an area in life where the psychological and the spiritual merge very neatly. Parents who understand this can enhance the spiritual growth of their children by the application of what we have to call psychological principles. Christian parents who are quite willing to acknowledge the role of the physician in physical illness consider that reliance on a psychologist or a psychiatrist is evidence of lack of faith in the Lord's ability to straighten matters out.

As familiar as I am with the surgical problems of children, I will never be able to accept with equanimity the physical and sexual abuse of children. No one in what we like to call "his right mind" would countenance such abusive behavior, yet there is a sense in which many well meaning parents "abuse" their children. Before you turn the page in disagreement, consider if you will how some of these things might be abusive to children in the long run:

8

- considering that a child has no rights;
- being so critical of a child that he has no self-esteem or, on the other hand,
- being so uncritical that the child has no guidelines;
- failing to let a youngster know that there is something unique about him;
- sharing your dissatisfaction or concern about your child with a group of friends (or perhaps even praying about them in public at the midweek church service);
- being inconsistent in the application of discipline;
- failing to be sensitive and protective of a child when he has exposed his innermost feelings;
- expecting behavior in a child that is inconsistent with your own.

In addition to being a pediatric surgeon, I am also a father. We had four children, three boys and a girl—in that order. Raising a child in an era of the confluence of women's lib, sexual freedom, and utilitarian philosophy is no easy task and parents need all the help they can get.

Not long ago I was at a professional-social function and walked up to a group of six of my peers only to realize that I must have interrupted a confidential conversation because silence fell on the group and I felt that I should move on. Indeed I did so only to have one of my friends reach out and pull me back and say: "Come back! There is no reason you should not know what we are talking about. We were just commenting that each of us is an assistant professor or better and that we have had not only the advantages of higher education but should know how to raise a family. Each of us has at least one child under psychiatric care."

As our children grew up, my wife and I realized we were walking a tightrope between permissiveness and control. Our third son went to be with the Lord at the age of 20, and his death was the occasion for his three siblings to recommit their lives to Jesus Christ and to reassess the urgency of making Him known. To have three solid Christian children married to three solid Christians raising three Christian families should be the expectation of any parent with multiple children. Sadly, the realization of this is not always the case.

An area of very practical temptation is that in which career and family compete for a parent's time. In the profession with which I am most familiar, I have seen a number of youngsters "go down the drain" because of their mother's assessment of their father in his role as father and husband. When a father must be away because of the demands made upon his time by his job, the mother must be ready to take the responsibility of both parents. She must not by word, deed, or innuendo let her children suspect that their father is anything less than the best father and husband.

It was with great delight that I read the manuscript of this book. I realized early on that Elizabeth Skoglund knew what she was talking about and was able to say it with great sensitivity. Not only sensitivity but practicality—without the rigidity of rules but with the flexibility of compromise that is a parent's obligation.

I like what I have read so much that as soon as this book is published, I plan to buy three copies for my children and their spouses. I know it would be most helpful in raising their own families.

C. Everett Koop, M.D., ScO.
Children's Hospital of Philadelphia

10

PREFACE

The day that, in the name of counseling, I held a child while she cried for one solid hour, and the times I have advised parents of babies with problems who were too young for counseling, convinced me that many children's emotional problems can be averted or solved by their own parents. All parents need is a basic understanding of children. *You Can Be Your Own Child's Counselor* is not meant to replace child therapy but rather to help prevent the need for it, or speed up the termination of such therapy.

Every parent provides a deeply formative influence for his child. In that way he *is* already his own child's therapist. This book is an attempt to improve the quality of do-it-yourself therapy.

1
ESTIMATING POTENTIAL

Eight-year-old Suzanne sat across from me in the coffee shop eating her hamburger, chatting happily about Christmas vacation. We had a warm relationship. I had known her for about six months now and in that short time she had grown from a fearful, shy child to one who was more comfortable at school and less hostile at home.

In the context of our relationship it was easy for me to relax and allow my thoughts to float back over my own past Christmas month. It had been grim, but I was once again okay and back into the usual swing of life. Six weeks earlier my father had undergone a massive stroke. Then a week before Christmas he died. I knew he was dying so, early in the Christmas season, I bought and decorated a spindly little tree which my mother and I halfheartedly picked out. I decorated it one night while she was visiting my father at the hospital. How happy she was when she saw the tree! She thought I had done it for my father when he would come home. I felt ambivalent: I did not want her to sense my pessimism yet I did not want to bolster her hopes for my father's recovery.

Suzanne's voice interrupted my thoughts. "Don't be so sad," she said quietly. "I know your father died, but you still have your family and friends."

Her sympathy and depth jolted me out of myself as I realized that her perception of me was pretty deep for an eight year old; and, after all, I was there to help her, not myself. Once again I focused back on Suzanne, but not before I recognized afresh the depth and understanding of life that even a child can possess.

Children Are Aware of Life's Problems

I have seen this potential so often as a child counselor. Children are not subhuman robots. To the contrary, while they often have immature perceptions of life, they observe life far more accurately than most of us suspect.

Everyone thought five-year-old Jo Ann didn't know what she was saying when she threatened suicide until she lighted herself up with matches and screamed. "I want to die, I want to die."

Kristine's parents thought it was a childish whim when she stated that she would never get married because she was afraid to have children. Yet when I talked to Kristine I found that she had a very definite reason: she didn't understand how a baby could be born through

14

such a small opening. A three-minute explanation of dilation dissolved her fears and she decided that children might not be so bad after all.

Ten-year-old Marcia wondered why nudity was wrong when God made us nude? Twelve-year-old Kent wanted to know when it was wrong to get angry and when it was right. Four-year-old Melissa told me I couldn't answer an emergency phone call because it was "her hour." She emphasized the point by stamping her foot.

Many adults treat children as though they had little consciousness of the world around them.

Two women sat on the beach talking while the little son of one of them played in the sand nearby. "I'm going to remarry soon," the mother said. "And I'm going to take my son with me." She nodded at the boy.

"Of course, he should go," her friend agreed.

"I'm not going with you!" the boy shouted. The women ignored him and continued talking. He shouted several more times. But only twice did the women even acknowledge him with a placating nod.

Children, Like Adults, Have Feelings and Opinions

Too often we ignore children as if they were insensitive. Whether we like it or not, children are individuals with unique personalities. They should be treated that way.

The practice of ignoring children is not new. People were doing it in Bible times. Even the disciples pushed them away. But Christ showed how highly He valued them when He said, "Suffer little children to come unto me, and forbid them not: for of such is the kingdom of God. Verily I say unto you, Whosoever shall not receive

15

the kingdom of God as a little child shall in no wise enter therein" (Luke 18:16,17, *KJV*).

How often we underestimate children. One small boy whom I counseled once a week before school seemed to enjoy his sessions. I presumed he went to school feeling a little happier. Actually the reverse was true. One day after his appointment he said to the secretary of the clinic where I worked at that time, "So far this has been a pretty good day. It seems a shame to ruin it by going to school."

However, the fact that children are perceptive in their thinking does not mean that they are adult in their understanding of life. By the time I met Janice she was nineteen and very disturbed. One facet of her disturbance was a deep hatred which she felt toward her mother and, apparently, had felt for years.

Now, years later, Janice told me about the night her father died from a heart attack. Janice was twelve. When her mother saw her husband go into his attack, she shoved Janice out of the room to protect her and reached for a bottle of medication. As Janice told me about the incident she and I realized that for all these years she had blamed her mother for her father's death, thinking that her mother had poisoned him with the pills. Clearing up that misconception did not cure Janice, but it helped. And the misunderstanding clearly illustrates that while children have a great depth of understanding they also need adult guidance in *interpreting* some of the information they gather.

Children Need Guidance in Figuring Out Life

It is in combining the childhood potential for understanding and growth with adult wisdom and warmth that parents can, at times, be their own child's therapist.

Late one afternoon a young mother called me, and in a rather frantic tone of voice explained her problem. Her eighteen-month-old baby had been hurt in an auto accident in recent weeks and the hospital treatment had added to the trauma of the accident. The little girl had to be put in restraints in order for the bones to heal, and she suffered a good deal of pain.

Now she was well physically but had begun to hit her head against her crib. The parents tried a sleeping harness, but even that failed to prevent her from bashing her head so violently that the doctor was afraid of the possibility of a skull fracture.

Eighteen months is just a little young for counseling! Furthermore, some things were fairly apparent to me even from the phone call. The harness was only increasing the child's anger. Frequently the parents would scold her or slap her hands when she was beating her head, again only further increasing the already present anger. In short, an angry, frightened child, who had been through a very terrifying experience, was just getting more angry and more frightened.

Rather than having the child come to my office, I suggested to the mother that the child was not "bad," she was angry—and justifiably so. Then I recommended that she stop *all* punitive measures like hand slapping, and every time the baby began hitting her head, that she or her husband pick her up and hold her. In a very short time the parents' love and the security had reduced her anger and modified her behavior so that the child stopped the self-destructive behavior altogether.

The action the parents could take in this case was far more effective than anything a professional person could have accomplished. The parents became the child's therapists.

Whether they want to accept it or not, *all* parents profoundly influence their children in the forming of their self-identity. The issue is not whether or not this influence exists but, rather, how effective in a positive way the influence will be. In the sense that therapists influence growth and change, *every parent is his or her own child's therapist.* The question is "How good will that therapy be?"

The Key to Helping Your Children Is a Positive Relationship

The vehicle waiting to be used to help your child is that of a good, positive relationship. An eight-year-old patient, Maria, showed me something of the ingredients of such a relationship.

Maria carefully arranged the furniture in the doll-house. The tiny doll children were put to bed, and the mother and father were propped up in chairs downstairs watching TV. Carefully Maria placed the dollhouse on the shelf and turned to choose a take-home toy from the toy box before she left my office. As she shuffled through the various dimestore toys, she looked up at me and said, "No one will play in here while I'm gone, will they? No one will change the dollhouse?" The counselor, the room in which she played, the toys, and especially the dollhouse, were hers for one hour a week and she didn't want to share them. She wanted to feel special, because being special imparts a sense of worth.

Any relationship has a variety of elements. Love, anger, trust, jealousy, boredom, selflessness, sharing are just some possibilities. But within the framework of all those facets, a relationship with any one person is unique, different in quality from that with any other person. Thus a child and his parent may share the same amount of love as another child and the same parent. But the quality of the relationship itself is special and cannot be duplicated.

Each child is uniquely loved, uniquely trusted, uniquely shared with, even uniquely disciplined. If his uniqueness with his parents is positive, the relationship contributes to a child's feeling of self-esteem. And unless something later in life reverses these feelings, the image the child forms of himself will stay with him throughout his life.

Every Child Needs a Good Self-Esteem

A good self-estimate, feelings of worth, is the focal point of what every child needs. Self-esteem is one of the most vital factors in determining a person's level of emotional health. Yet, particularly within Christian groups, it is often a grossly misunderstood concept.

Self-esteem is the value one places on his own personal worth. Consciously or unconsciously, we all evaluate ourselves. To have self-esteem means that we like ourselves or are comfortable with ourselves. In no way does such a viewpoint mean that we become complacent or unwilling to change or unable to see faults that need correction. But it does imply considerable self-acceptance.

Partly because we have distorted the words "conceited" and "humble," we have confused the scriptural viewpoint of self-worth. To be conceited means to be so unsure of your own worth that you must constantly remind yourself, and the world, of your greatness. To be truly humble means to have an honest evaluation of your worth, realizing good and bad points, and to possess a degree of contentedness about your self.

C.S. Lewis (in *Mere Christianity*) describes the humble man in the same way that one could describe a man with a good self-image. "He will not be a sort of greasy, smarmy person, who is always telling you that, of course, he is nobody. Probably all you will think about him is that he seemed a cheerful, intelligent chap who took a real interest in what *you* said to *him*. If you do dislike him, it will be because you feel a little envious of anyone who seems to enjoy life so easily. He will not be thinking about humility: he will not be thinking of himself at all."[1]

For the Christian, the issue of self-esteem merges the psychological and the spiritual in a way that sometimes makes the one indistinguishable from the other. Faith in Christ and in His giving of His Spirit to us, makes us vastly important, for it is God who declares us important. In Luke 12:6,7 Christ says, "What is the price of five sparrows? A couple of pennies? Not much more than that. Yet God does not forget a single one of them. And he knows the number of hairs on your head! Never fear, you are far more valuable to him than a whole flock of sparrows."

But if faith in God and knowledge of His viewpoint toward us increases our potential for proper self-esteem, there is a parallel psychological truth. Faith in one's worth often makes it easier to trust in God's care for us. I once heard a minister say, "A person who dislikes himself may end up with psychological problems, but he will probably be a better Christian because he will trust God more."

Such a statement is false and misleading. I have had teenagers and adults alike tell me that they cannot trust God or ask Him for help because "How could God care" about them? They honestly believe that no one, especially God, could really love them. It is often necessary to help such people raise their self-esteem before their religious faith can be of any help to them. Thus psychological strength should help make us better Christians, while being a Christian should also increase our psychological strength.

The Bible Teaches About Self-Esteem

There is biblical evidence for the rightness of a proper self-image. Paul on several occasions shows pleasure over his accomplishments. In Romans 15:17,18 he says, "So it is right for me to be a little proud of all Christ Jesus has done through me. I dare not judge how effectively he has used others, but I know this: he has used me to win the Gentiles to God." Again in Romans 12:6 Paul says, "God has given each of us the ability to do certain things well." The obvious implication is that we are to be aware of our strengths and appreciate them.

But self-esteem is more than just liking certain isolated characteristics about ourselves. Thus, at the end of his life, Paul could say to Timothy, "I have fought long and hard for my Lord, and through it all I have kept true to him" (2 Tim. 4:7). He expresses a contentment that is appropriate and right.

Just the fact that God is a God of truth is evidence enough of God's approval of us when we have a good honest estimate of ourselves. It is not a virtue to say that I am not good at my job, if I am good at it. Nor is it right to deny any other good point about myself. Self-esteem, to be real, must be based on an honest evaluation of oneself. To be dishonest is certainly not Christian.

A teenage girl who is a brilliant pianist told me that, while she knows she's good at playing the piano, she feels wrong about her awareness of that ability. Sometimes she goes so far as to try to play poorly so that she won't be so proud! Understandably, this drives her teacher to distraction and is not in the end a very good example of Christianity.

Low self-esteem doesn't make anyone appealing to others and it becomes the height of self-occupation, which is the very thing the Bible speaks against. People who dislike themselves are not humble, they are self-occupied. They are continually concentrating on their failure, their supposed lack of worth. In contrast, people who like themselves are self-forgetful.

One seventh-grade girl who, because of her low self-image, hates social situations, goes home after a party and rehearses the whole evening in her mind. She, of course, always comes out looking badly to herself.

Thus a person with low self-esteem frequently spends painful hours concentrating on real or, more often, imagined slights and criticisms from those around him. Indeed, he is so occupied with himself that he can hardly pay any attention at all to others. Yet paying attention to those around us is a primary scriptural command.

Christians Should See Their Own Self-Worth in Perspective

It is true that the Bible speaks much about the sinfulness of man and his nothingness apart from God. John 15:5 says, "Without me ye can do nothing" *(KJV)*. Before a sinless, all-powerful God, man certainly falls very short. But this is a spiritual problem having a spiritual answer in Christ's redemption. Furthermore, as a Christian progresses in his spiritual life, he will function spiritually by spiritual laws. Yet viewing ourselves among other men, it is right to see our strengths and talents as finite human beings.

One evening as I was chatting with friends, one man who was extremely successful in business turned to me and said, "Without God, I could not do my job. Each day I give myself anew to Him for His power and direction." In a sort of paradoxical way, he was completely accurate. He is a close friend and I believe him to be one of the strongest persons, psychologically, that I know. He's sure of himself. While he doesn't enjoy rejection or slights, he doesn't lose any sleep over them either when they do occur. When he has an idea at work, he has the confidence to pursue and promote it. Socially, he's liked and likable. Yet he echoes the idea in John 15 that apart from God he can do nothing. His spiritual and psychological sides are beautifully integrated. For ultimately no man on this earth takes a breath of air apart from the grace of God. And, more specifically, no man, no matter how strong, can do a work for God without God.

However, accepting the fact that it is all right to have self-esteem in no way guarantees its possession. The fact that it is so hard to come by is proven by how hard most of us seem to struggle to get and maintain it.

How Do Children Get a Good Self-Esteem?

Self-esteem is based, first of all, on the reality of one's behavior. If I am behaving in a way that I can respect, and can perceive my behavior accurately, this will boost my self-image. Here again, rather than being contradictory, psychology and Christianity complement each other. The Bible describes Christian behavior as it should be. This is perhaps best summarized in John 13:34,35: "A new commandment I give unto you, That ye love one another; as I have loved you, that ye also love one another. By this shall all men know that ye are my disciples, if ye have love one to another" *(KJV)*.

When people follow such a standard for living, they tend to like themselves better. A little boy who usually had a messy closet became aware of his mother's hurt after his father died suddenly in an accident. One evening he came quietly over to her and said, "You should see my closet, Mommy." Then he showed her a row of neat shoes and a rack of clothes that had been carefully hung up. He continued, "I decided that if I'm going to be the head of the house, things should look better." Happy, he then went off to bed. He liked himself a little better because he had done an act of love. What we do and what we are gives us a basis for what we think of ourselves.

But the problem becomes more complicated. Some people cannot see their worth. No matter how good they are, they think they're bad. A child with a bright mind will look at a simple math problem and, without trying, say, "I can't do it." A pretty teenage girl will say, "I'm too ugly to be asked out by that boy." A twelve-year-old boy will sit in my office and say, "But if you really knew me, you wouldn't like me at all."

Sometimes the manifestation of low self-esteem is not so obvious. Low self-esteem generates anxiety which in turn may produce seemingly unrelated symptoms. The businessman suffering from an ulcer or the housewife who feels frequent attacks of anxiety may really be suffering from a lack of self-esteem. The girl who has a fear of elevators and the young woman who has frequent headaches may also be able to trace their surface problem to their sense of self-worth.

What is significant for our consideration is that a number of adverse situations during these people's formative years probably account for their lack of accuracy in perceiving their own worth. Usually children develop their self-image at a very young age and usually the parents are very influential. That is the very basic reason why the formation of a good relationship in a child is so important.

All of us, at all ages, tend to at least partially evaluate our worth by the relationships we have with those around us. If I am loved, I begin to feel lovable, especially if the person who loves me is someone I consider worthwhile.

A young child requires relationships that are sincere and fairly constant. A basic ingredient of all emotional difficulties is the problem of low self-esteem. One of the best antidotes is a good relationship. It is therefore imperative that if we are to raise emotionally healthy children, the places where they live the most, the home and school, must provide constructive relationships with responsible adults.

Even though no one would blame a child who was abandoned, many children in that situation blame themselves. Small children have told me that if they were "good" their parent would move back home. Thus, a parent's absence lowered the child's self-image in an unrealistic way.

Children will often go out of their way to defend a parent and blame themselves instead. Jenny was eight when I first saw her. Abandoned by her parents because they were strung out on drugs and really didn't want her, Jenny still defended them. They were too busy, their life was hard enough without her. Someday they would come back. But the effect on her self-esteem was profound. Her relationships with the adult world had proven themselves to be insecure, and so she blamed herself. She had uncontrollable fits of crying and kicking until, exhausted, she fell asleep. With the help of counseling where the relationship could be depended on and a caring foster home, the crying and kicking stopped. The last I heard she was seemingly developing into a self-confident ten-year-old.

Besides being dependable, if a relationship with a child is to be constructive in building self-esteem, it must be positive. Children who hear about how bad the neighbors are, and how badly most children behave, will begin to personalize such feelings and believe that if everyone is that bad, they must be bad, too. A child who is bright, but who is never told that he is because it will "make him vain," may grow up genuinely unaware of his high intelligence. A child who is not told that he is loved and wanted, may begin to believe he is in the way.

Melissa was a twelve-year-old girl who saw me for a while because her parents were sure that she was turning into a juvenile delinquent like her brother. One day she said in all seriousness, "Why should I even try to go to school and succeed? I'm no good. Even my mother doesn't want me."

I quickly objected, saying I was sure she had misinterpreted her mother's feelings. Two weeks later her mother said to me, "Neither Melissa's father nor I want her anymore. Where can we send her?"

When I saw Melissa that last time I didn't have to say anything, even though her parents had not yet told her of their decision. She just looked at me and quietly and sadly said, "I told you they didn't want me. They've never wanted any of us kids."

How do you prove to a twelve-year-old girl that it's her parents' messed-up lives that are at fault, not hers? How do you tell her about her own worth when the world she's closest to has rejected her?

Children must be liked and loved in an open, clear way. Then they will probably grow up liking themselves. However, the love a child gets in his early relationships must be discriminating. To tell Johnny that all he does is good when he knows that's not true, makes him lose faith in your judgment altogether. As one boy said, "Oh, my mother. She doesn't count. According to her, everything I do is wonderful."

Is it a sin to like yourself? No. But it is closer to sin to raise a child so that he can't see his own good points and his own worth. Romans 12:3,5 tell us to "be honest in your estimate of yourselves . . . so we belong to each other, and each needs all the others."

In Summary

1. Realize that children are very aware of what is going on around them. They hear their parents and others talking about problems and, often without enough information, they form their own feelings and opinions.

2. Keep channels of conversation open between you and your children, so that they will feel comfortable discussing their anger, fears and confusion.

3. Establish a relationship with each child, uniquely

for that child. He must realize that he is special, different in his own way and accepted for who he is. Your relationships must be dependable and positive.

Note

1. C.S. Lewis, *Mere Christianity* (New York: Macmillan Publishing Co., 1964), p. 114.

2
BUILDING TRUST

Eleven-year-old Susan suddenly became quieter than usual. We had been talking about her progress in school and about her brother's new girl friend.

"Why am I coming here?" she asked. And then before I could answer her she continued, "My grades are better and I don't fight as much at home. But I still wish I were a boy. I hate being a girl—and that's a problem, isn't it?"

We had talked for many months. I had listened. I had not repeated confidences to her mother. I had not caused her to be punished. I had respected her wishes and her opinions. Now she could really trust me with one of the deepest awarenesses she had of herself. Later there came the day when she came into my office saying: "I've decided I like being a girl and I want my hair to look like yours." But for this earlier day she trusted me with her first glimmer of painful knowledge that at this time in her life she did not feel like other girls she knew.

That trust had become the outgrowth of a number of facets of our relationship, qualities that should be true of any parent-child relationship.

A Child Will Trust You When You Respect His Rights

Children often have no rights. Parents sometimes listen in on their child's conversation, search through his room when he isn't home, or tell him "children should be seen and not heard" when he voices an opinion. An adult who is fearful of water is encouraged to try to swim or at least get into the water. Children are more likely to be forced in because they are physically too little to resist. Even our adoption laws seem to protect the rights of the parent to change his mind more than they do the child who is shunted from one foster home to another while the parent vacillates in his decision regarding the child's custody.

When parents respect their children's rights, the children, in turn, learn to respect their parents' rights. No child should be allowed to trample over the rights of his parents. Parents need time alone with each other if their marriage is to remain intact. They have the right to feelings of all kinds as long as they don't hurt their children with inappropriate expression of those feelings.

If you don't listen in on your child's conversation with his friend, you teach him to give you the same right to privacy. If you respect his possessions you teach him to respect those of others. Respect his right to disagree with your thinking at times and he will be more inclined to hear your side when he disagrees with you. Especially as he grows up and has greater potential for freedom, he will by choice continue to give you the right to disagree with him and will hear your point of view. Within the boundaries of respect, good relationships flourish.

A very angry ten-year-old boy came to see me for a while. He was constantly in trouble for his angry outbursts and was told he shouldn't act that way. My office was the one place in his life where he could freely express his anger—usually in a verbal way while he pounded away at a toy that couldn't be broken. In one of the early sessions he continued showing his anger for almost the whole hour. Then toward the end, a sudden quietness came over him. He looked up at me from the floor where he was seated and politely said, "I'm sorry to have been so noisy. I guess it's time to leave. Have a good day."

As I walked with him to the door, I felt a warmth over the respect that we had for each other. I showed respect in allowing him to express feelings that were very real to him. I gave him the *right* to be angry and to express that anger appropriately. He showed respect for my rights by never personalizing his anger toward me, an innocent person who was not responsible for creating his problems. Such was not the case outside of my office. Whenever someone rebuked him for his feelings, he was capable of turning his anger on them in a way that they did not really deserve. But when he was treated with the dignity due any person, he returned the treatment. He returned the rights he was given.

Being allowed to have basic rights builds a feeling of dignity and an awareness of our own uniqueness. One of the most succinct statements of the uniqueness of a human being is given by Fabry in his book about Viktor Frankl, *Pursuit of Meaning*. Fabry says of Frankl's teachings that "each person is unique—he lives his unique life, has his unique opportunities and potentials, but also his unique shortcomings; he creates his unique relationships with others and accepts his unique tasks; he faces his unique sufferings, experiences his unique guilt feelings, and dies his unique death."[1]

Such uniqueness is true of an individual from birth on. A child's relationships at home, and to some extent those at school, help determine whether he feels his uniqueness in a positive or negative way. Children, unlike adults, must be given the right to be unique since they cannot successfully just take that right. To know which rights to give a child and which ones he should be denied remains the responsibility of every parent. To always say no or to always be permissive may be easier for the parent but is also damaging to a child. To find a balance is harder but it results in a healthier child.

Respecting the Child's Rights to Privacy Builds Trust

Privacy implies respect and respect implies a sense of worth and trust. One can only have feelings of closeness toward a person who brings out such feelings of worth. I will often say to a child whom I see for the first time, "There is no reason why you should trust me yet, for you don't know me. In time I hope you will. But until then we will talk about things you feel comfortable talking about. I will not try to intrude into your feelings any further than you wish me to." The child feels a sense of worth by having his privacy thus respected.

The most obvious breach of such privacy is when a

parent goes through his child's purse or drawer, throws away a favorite doll or shirt, or listens in on his conversations. Equally bad is betraying his confidences or pointing out his weaknesses in front of others. A fifteen-year-old girl told me how, when her aunt asked her how her job was going, her mother interrupted with, "What job? She's never there." The girl was angry because she not only felt betrayed, but her mother's answer made the situation sound worse than it really was. The same girl was upset because the whole church knew about her problems because her parents "wanted them to pray."

Parents have the right to confide in their close friends or family members when they feel that need. If they are Christians, they will want some prayer support. And if they feel peculiarly justified in looking through a purse or a drawer because they know their son or daughter is on drugs, they should do so. But all these actions must be carefully weighed before they are done, for in general every human being at all ages has a right and need for privacy. A parent who ignores that need thoughtlessly too often tears down his child's trust in him.

The parent who does not demand that his child confide in him, but offers to be there when he is needed, is allowing his son or daughter the dignity of privacy and at the same time offering the closeness of a good relationship. When a twelve-year-old girl broke up her relationship with her best friend she didn't want to talk about it at first. Her mother tactfully said, "I understand your not wanting to talk yet. But when you're ready, let me know." Later that day they talked, but it was at the girl's timing. She did not feel intruded upon, but at the same time she knew that in her mother she had someone who cared.

33

Parents Need to Help Children Trust God

Spiritual trust in a child, based on a background of good biblical training, is vital in the Christian family. A child needs to feel his uniqueness in his own relationship with God.

In some Christian circles today it is popular to feel that a child of any age is always to be controlled by his parents' decisions. This viewpoint seems to be contradicted by verses like Matthew 8:21,22 where a disciple of Christ says to Him, " 'Sir, when my father is dead, then I will follow you.' But Jesus told him, 'Follow me *now*'!" In Luke 14:26 Christ says, "Anyone who wants to be my follower must love me far more than he does his own father, mother, wife, children, brothers, or sisters—yes, more than his life—otherwise he cannot be my disciple."

The implication of these passages seems to be that a young person, while he is to honor his parents, should increasingly place himself under the direct authority of God rather than under his parents' interpretation of that authority. Parents should instill in their child the knowledge that he is free under God, free to exercise his spiritual will as he sees it to be right. A child who grows up with a good image of himself learns to make responsible decisions as an adult. And it is important that the parent see his role as the one who helps the child develop into this independent human being who accepts himself and has a healthy individual relationship with God.

No child is the property of his parents. During the years of their development they are a trust from God to be guided and loved. They are not to be tyrannized over like some robot with no thoughts of their own any more than we as adults are puppets under a God who capriciously pulls the strings and forces our obedience.

While children need direction and control in order to build up feelings of security, they also need to be taught to make their own choices in order to become independent adults with a good self-image. A parent who sits down every night and "helps" his child do his homework is not helping him build independence and good self-esteem. Certainly the parent should be available for questions, but I do not approve of the rather large numbers of parents who practically do the homework themselves.

A mother should honestly discuss the problem of premarital sex with her teenage daughter, but she is behaving in a destructive way if she *unreasonably* restricts the girl's dating in order to insure her safety. It is an unalterable fact of life that once a child reaches a certain age his behavior cannot be controlled. Parents and others who are in a position of influence should teach the child in such a way that, by the time he is old enough to make some decisions of his own, he will make responsible decisions. At that point he will be able to determine for himself such things as what career to pursue and who to marry. These decisions are primarily between him and God. By the time a young person reaches late teens and early adulthood his parents should be in an advisory rather than a controlling position. And the growing child who has been trusted will usually make wiser decisions than the one who has never been taught and trusted to make his own choices.

The Christian parent who has a healthy relationship with God will be able to relate that spirituality to his children in a way that will increase their strength. There is a world of difference between the child who is taught that God will strike him dead if he crosses his parents' will and the child who turns to God for protection when he is afraid because he has seen his parents do it.

God made it clear in the Bible that certain things are wrong—like stealing, gossiping and pride. But far too often even small children become guilt-ridden or turn off God because Christianity has been presented to them as a list of rules instead of a relationship with a loving God. When the mother of a seventeen-year-old boy asked me if she should force him to go to church, my answer was no. By now if his resistance to church was that strong, sheer force would probably only deepen his feelings. Whereas if he was allowed to make his own decision, hopefully he would someday overcome his resentment and be able to develop his own relationship to God.

It is, of course, far better if the parent can keep such resentment from developing, for a relationship with God is not only vital spiritually but it adds to one's emotional health. When a twelve-year-old boy was becoming rebellious in a Christian private school his parents brought him to see me. His rebellion was based largely on some of the school rules, rules the public school did not have. He was not yet rebelling against God or Christianity, just the school. I strongly advised that he be put in a public school in order to preserve the positive Christian attitude he still had. The change proved successful. His hostility was lowered and his attitude toward life in general became more healthy and positive.

Far too often Christianity is used as a club with young people, a way of keeping them from deviating from their parents' standards. In contrast, Christianity is really meant to be very positive. A young child, who had been told that her mother and father didn't want her, was placed in a Christian foster home. Not long after that she came into my office bubbling over with happiness because she had learned about a God who loved her. Between the positive Christian teaching, the warmth of an unusually good foster home, and the effects of counseling, a very disturbed little girl became happier and calmer in a relatively short period of time.

Particularly with preteens and teenagers one has to be careful to present Christ in all His aspects, not just the sterner side. As one thirteen-year-old girl said when overly strict rules were being thrown at her from a well meaning Christian, "I wish I weren't a Christian so I could do what was best for me." What a sad statement when one realizes that what is best for us is exactly what God wants for us. Instead of being helped by her Christian faith, inaccurate teaching—in the name of Christ—was causing greater problems in her.

Trust Results in Spiritual and Psychological Strength

If a child knows his parents increasingly put more trust in him as he grows in the spiritual realm, he not only becomes spiritually stronger but he is also psychologically more sound. For trust in general breeds responsibility. Goethe's idea is true that if we treat people as they are they become worse, but if we treat them as though they were what they are capable of becoming we help them reach their full potential. Trust says, "I know you can make it."

Trust is the basic ingredient of any good relationship and positive relationships are the foundation for a child's good self-image. And, in essence, only too often people *do* become what we expect them to become. Trust is essential to a good counseling relationship. The counselor respects the privacy and rights of his patient and recognizes his uniqueness. The child is expected to grow and to change. Yet that growth increasingly becomes the child's own responsibility, not that of the therapist. He is trusted. So it must be for the parent and his child.

In Summary

1. A good counselor establishes a relationship of trust with those he counsels. Your child will learn to trust you when you:

- respect his rights to his own possessions;
- respect his rights to his own opinions;
- respect his rights to express his feelings and emotions;
- honor his right to private conversations with his friends;
- keep confidences he shares with you;
- help him build his sense of self worth;
- teach him to trust himself.

2. While teaching your child to always honor his parents, also teach him to freely choose to place himself under the direct authority of God. Your child will learn to trust God if you:

- model a healthy relationship with God;
- set examples of trust in God.

Note

1. Joseph B. Fabry *Pursuit of Meaning* (Boston: Beacon Press, Inc., 1969).

3
COMMUNICATING IN A RELATIONSHIP

Amy was hitting her brother and pounding on the door of my waiting room while I attempted to finish a session with a patient in my office. When I finally opened my door I saw a very unhappy, angry little girl hunched up in a chair with a knitted stocking cap pulled down over her face. She scowled as her brother Tommy asked if he could come in and play too. That was all she needed!

Amy's father had recently died and her mother had started work full time. A new school, new apartment and new friends—or in her case no friends—had almost been too much for Amy to handle. She was angry at the world and herself and hoping to secure someone who would not disappear or disappoint her.

Sensing her special need on this day to get away from even the presence of her mother and brother with whom she competed for attention, I took Amy to a local coffee shop and we started to talk. The result was incredible. Amy *did* talk. She relaxed. She felt safe and special. I found out that when she was angry she had learned to take out her feelings by hitting other children or yelling at them, predictably the response was that of rejection. We talked about what she was doing and how it was bad. Not that *she* was a bad person, but that what she was doing was bringing pain to herself as well as to other people.

"I want people to like me," Amy finally admitted. "But they make me so angry."

Listening Is Essential to Good Communication

Setting had been vital in getting Amy to talk. On that day she needed a quiet, private place with someone all to herself who cared about her. Such a setting, combined with real listening, is basic to any clear kind of verbal communication.

Often someone has come to my office, talked rapidly for an hour, and scarcely given me a chance to say anything. Yet because I cared and listened, the person felt better when he left. No great exchange of information had transpired. But someone listened.

One of the most helpful things a parent can do is listen. Listening to anyone is very ego-inflating, for it involves the giving of the most precious thing any of us own—a part of ourselves, our time, our lives.

In counseling, listening is a pivotal aspect of success. Most children and teenagers put high value in the fact that their hour with me is their time to do and say as they please. A teenage boy described his free hour to his friend in the following words: "Man, it's really great! Why go where the pigs tell you to go? As long as you have to go why not go where it's going to do you some good? Man, it's really great. If you want to break things, kick, scream or just sit and cry, it's your time and she really hears you." The value of a special time of listening is further shown by the comments of small children who, when they are reaching the end of the hour, say things like, "Can I still talk a little more?" or, "Are you sure that clock is working?" or, "How much longer do I have?"

A seven-year-old boy was sent to visit his uncle in another state. Timmy had never met the uncle but cheerfully told me of his intended visit the week before. When he returned three weeks later his mother brought him in to see me.

He sat moodily in my office and refused to talk. Finally when I asked him why, he replied, "I won't talk as long as my mother is waiting out there," and he pointed to the waiting room. We solved the problem by going to a coffee shop where, over a glass of root beer, Timmy told me of his traumatic three weeks. His parents told him that he was going on a short trip to visit his uncle. He was a little apprehensive and asked questions like, "Will you come with me?" and, "How long will I stay?" No one seemed to hear him, so he arrived at his own conclusions. Short meant only for a day—and not very far away. And of course his parents would either accompany him or meet him when he got there.

When Timmy was put on the plane in the care of a stewardess, he got a little frightened. But it was not until he arrived at his uncle's and saw that his parents were not there, that the truth began to dawn on him. Not only was he alone but he was given a bed and told that he would stay many nights.

To the adult mind, the mistake was ridiculous. Everyone knows you wouldn't fly to another state and come home again the same day. And how could his father leave his business and his mother leave a small baby? Logical to an adult mind? Yes. But no one stopped to listen to his questions and try to understand the logic of a child's mind that thought "short" was a few hours, and his parents would of course be with him.

Listening is a basic problem in many homes. It always takes time. And sometimes it doesn't seem necessary to take the time, as in Timmy's case, where everyone assumed what seemed obvious to them. But no family can ever be really together without taking time to listen to one another.

I often advise parents to spend individual time with each child and listen to him: a father and son at a ball game, a mother and daughter shopping for clothes, Saturday morning breakfast in a restaurant or Sunday night ice cream at home can provide a setting of one-to-one privacy in which any parent can really hear what his child is feeling. Such times will help form deep, formative relationships but they must be hedged in with safeguards.

Proper Discipline Creates Communication

Perhaps the area most precarious in an adult/child relationship is the area of discipline. I use discipline rather than punishment because discipline includes both the negative and the positive which will foster good behavior in the future. Punishment implies retribution, getting even, an eye-for-an-eye type of reasoning.

When a child is disciplined, it should also be done on an individual basis. When I was out for dinner one night with a friend and her three children, one of them, Jason, misbehaved continuously. In her anger and embarrassment my friend said, "Can't you children behave? Next time I'll leave you all home." Actually, *one* child was causing the trouble and the other two were exercising considerable restraint. Two were disciplined unfairly and felt angry. The offending child was treated as though he were just part of a mass rather than as an individual who deserved individual attention.

A better handling of the situation would have been to take Jason aside and tell him that unless his conduct improved, he would not be taken out again until he could show that he was capable of behaving in a restaurant. It would be wrong to say, "You can't go with us again for a month." That would simply mean that Jason, whether he was bad or good, was restricted for an arbitrary period of time. But if he knows that eating in a restaurant depends on his behavior, it leaves the controls to him.

Often there may be instantaneous improvement because there is an incentive for such improvement. Or what might take Jason one month to learn could take his brother only a day or a week. That is the reason why discipline should vary from child to child, for each child is different. For some, a reprimand is quite sufficient, but others take more strict measures. Also what is true of one child at one time, may not be true of the same child at another time.

Whatever disciplinary dealings you may have with a child, the child needs to feel that the goal of that discipline is change in his actions or attitudes, it is not an angry release of adult feelings. When I was teaching I found that controlling a class of 35 students was very difficult at first. When they would talk, I would become angry and hand out demerits or make them stay after school. Nothing in my action changed their behavior, and it was a constant war.

Then I discovered that if I shifted the responsibility of their behavior from me to them, I had almost no discipline problems. First, together in a group discussion, we established what was a fair expectation. We decided it was fair, for example, to let one person talk without ten others interrupting. We decided that group discussions and individual projects added to the fun and effectiveness of learning. Therein lay the responsibility. We would use these more flexible methods of teaching as long as a given class could handle the added freedom —and most did. Behavior improved remarkably because the rules were fair and they had everything to lose from breaking them.

There was little need for discipline because most students wanted to go along with the rules. Any disciplinary methods that were needed were aimed at restoring the class and the individual to the degree of freedom and learning the students liked best. In the same way, the child who misbehaved in the restaurant should be disciplined with the goal of changing his behavior so he can eat in restaurants, which is probably the same goal he would want. This is in contrast to punishment that is applied to get even with the child for annoying the adult.

Children Should Be Allowed to Talk Freely
Verbal communication between a child and an adult

44

needs to follow certain ground rules. One of these rules is that when parents perceive that a child has a deep need to talk, they should remove all possibility of retribution in order for the child to feel he can voice his thoughts freely. With the amount of anger Amy felt, as we discussed at the outset of this chapter, punishment would have only increased her anger. Understanding and constructive advice were more effective in actually changing her behavior. There are times with their parents when children need these kinds of safety zones or safety periods.

In order to establish a relationship of trust, parent and child must both anticipate what the parent will do if the child reveals some act of misbehavior to him. Then the child will not feel betrayed. Furthermore, the child must feel that when he wants something kept secret, that trust will be respected. A seven-year-old child was describing to me the circumstances surrounding his running away from home a few weeks previous. What he was saying made the whole episode more understandable than it had seemed at first. When I asked him if he had told his parents these details, he said, "No, because when I ask them if they will tell anyone they don't answer. When I ask you, you promise not to. So I tell you."

During this time a parent spends alone with his child it is important not to push. Let him test you and talk at his own speed. A nine-year-old girl asked me a multitude of questions about how I had felt toward my parents when I was her age and what other children felt before she came out with the statement, "I hate my parents." As soon as she realized I was not going to reject her, our relationship grew rapidly and her hostility diminished.

A parent who really wants an honest relationship with his child must be a little shockproof, for he will at times hear things he would prefer not to hear. One teenage girl accused her mother of taking out her hostility toward her brother on her. This is a hard thing to hear but the mother was strong enough to see that her daughter was right. As a result all three of them have a better relationship and there is less hostility in that home.

In a sense, all of these methods of communication make the child feel good about himself because they have an underlying thread of dignity and respect and they will provoke dignity and respect from the child. On an even more specific level, they convey the feeling that parents accept children as people with depth.

Parents Need to Share Problems and Joys with Children

A child can reach out in understanding you more deeply than the average adult realizes. When his capacity for communication on various levels is developed it enhances his image of himself as well as his relationship with the adult world who trusts him in this special way. One of these levels is in the area of family problems.

One member of a family had a major illness. The children were protected from what was happening and were catered to as though life was normal. Yet it was not normal. If they had been given a few added responsibilities and a gentle but honest explanation of what was going on, the whole family would have been drawn closer together and each of them would have had a greater sense of the worth that comes from being needed. Instead, because the children had only snatches of information, they built up a distorted view of what was happening. They did not learn the joy of helping during a crisis. They did not feel needed or trusted.

There is a danger, of course, of giving children too much responsibility during difficult times. A six-year-old girl who cooks dinner for her working mother, and an eight-year-old boy who is told that he is now head of the family, are both being given adult responsibilities at too early an age. There is a delicate balance between what will make a child feel greater self-worth and increased closeness to others, and what will be a burden or a cause of unrealistic fear to him.

Problems are not all that should be shared. Happiness too should be shared. Tell your child about your promotion at work. Let him know when you're happy, even more than you let him know when you have a headache or have had a bad day. A very young child and I sat in my office one afternoon and talked about the books we had read—books like *Heidi, Little House on the Prairie, The Little Colonel.* I got drawn into the rather unusual conversation when I realized that this very bright and sensitive child wanted to share her joy in reading with me and, even more, wanted me to tell her about the books I had enjoyed as a child. At the end of the hour we were closer than we had ever been when we just discussed her problem. My sharing at her level drew us closer because we had interests in common as children, and because I as an adult took the time and interest to listen as well as to share my own feelings.

For Christians the spiritual area is another source of positive sharing. Too many Christian parents use Christianity as a club or a reason why a child can't do something. Christian standards are fine, as long as they're really Christian and not man-made laws. But why not share all the positive aspects of being a Christian? Let your children know when God answers your prayers or helps you through a hard spot. Let them know that Christianity is knowing, loving and serving Christ, not just following rules. Let them tell you about their spiritual experiences, and don't forget how much value Christ put on the faith of a child.

A little girl of seven who had been abandoned by her parents sat in my office one morning and cheerfully asked me if I knew God. When I said yes she chatted on about her new discovery in Sunday School—that she could pray to God and that He loved her. She was delighted to find a sympathetic listener.

Respect for Privacy Is Part of Communication

Every child and adult is entitled to privacy of feelings for that too makes him feel special. Sharing our fears and joys is great but it should not be forced. I can still remember with resentment the number of people who asked me if I was "saved" at an age when I was too little and shy to get rid of them. If God had not made Himself real to me, in spite of their intrusion into my privacy, they could have really turned me off to God. And as far as a relationship was concerned, their treatment of me made me withdraw from them rather than get close to them.

We need to respect the feelings of all members of a family, no matter how old or how young. A seven-year-old boy came into my office one day with a dejected, depressed expression on his face. When I gently probed to find out what was wrong, he just crawled deeper into his shell. So I suggested that we play his favorite game. Even that didn't help at first. Then at last he smiled. He never told me what happened because he didn't choose to, not because I wouldn't listen. But because I tolerated his privacy, even in feelings, he relaxed and began to relate to me over something he liked doing.

There is a closeness that one feels in just knowing that another person respects and loves you enough not to pry. Sometimes we don't want to share, and that feeling should be respected. A good relationship tolerates privacy.

Sometimes we need to know when *not* to verbally communicate.

Ultimately the parent must do what the professional counselor does. He must try as best he can, with the help of certain knowledge and guidelines, to verbally communicate with the deep but still unknown world of a child. For a child is a strange combination of depth and innocence, understanding and naivete, strength and weakness. His personality, even more than that of the adult, is at best marvelously resilient, at worst fragile and delicate. Its potential for strength must be reinforced, its possibility for destruction respected.

In Summary

1. Take time to listen, on a one-to-one basis, to what your child has to say.

2. Your discipline methods should be unique, according to the child's personality and disposition.

3. Allow your child the right to feel that he can voice his opinions and express his emotions freely, without fear of being punished.

4. Share with your children when your family faces problems or crises. The children need to learn the joy of helping during times of stress.

49

5. Share happy times, when good things happen to you.

6. Share spiritual things—answers to prayer, love of Christ and spiritual experiences.

7. Never insist that your child share with you unless he wants to.

4
TALKING WITHOUT WORDS

A little three-year-old girl was carefully making a "snowman" out of clay. She became intensely involved and so I let my mind drift away from her to the things I needed to do before I left my office.

Before I realized it, she was looking at me intently. Then with a dark scowl on her face she crushed the snowman in her hands, sat back and said, "I can't do anything right." Words had not conveyed that message to her, for there had been no words; nor had my actions been intended to relate to her. But to a child who already felt insecure, seeming apathy and indifference on my part reinforced feelings of low self-esteem as effectively as if I had spoken words of rejection.

I remembered another time when a seven-year-old child was taken by her mother and friends to an elaborate Sunday brunch where children of that age are not often seen. While the adults were served champagne, Christy was offered *two* Shirley Temples and was treated with great warmth by the waitress. Finally she was given a glass of milk with her dessert which she later described to a friend as being "served in a glass with a stem on it." The pleasantness of the waitress, the party atmosphere, Christy's long dress and the adult treatment which she experienced all combined to make her feel very important in spite of the fact that no one told her she was important. When she came home that night Christy was overheard telling her best friend: "I went to this beautiful place for brunch today. They took me because I'm special."

Children respond very strongly to stimuli other than words. By these nonverbal cues, they not only interpret other people's feelings toward them but also form their ideas about other people. This fact presents parents and educators with vital tools in working with children. Facial expression, tone of voice, touch, color and a myriad of other factors greatly influence children when words are never spoken or even in spite of what is said.

A Physical Atmosphere Communicates

Children respond to a physical atmosphere even though they may not be consciously aware of the specifics of that atmosphere. In developing a playroom where I work with disturbed children, I put in the room colorful pictures, attractive but durable furniture, and a variety of things to play with. Children who visit me have freedom to explore this atmosphere without adult intervention. The total environment seems to produce a very relaxing effect in many children. It is their room, geared to their tastes. I am careful not to include furniture or

toys that can be easily broken or are potentially danger-
ous. This is the method in which I minimize the need for
restrictions.

The effect was obvious one day when one little boy
asked, "Could I move in here for a while—with my two
friends—and maybe with my Mommy?" Another child,
the son of a friend of mine, said to his mother, "Can't
I go and visit Miss Skoglund each week? That's a neat
office and I'm sure I have problems I could talk about."
We convinced him that he could survive without counseling but he remains fascinated with the thought of
visiting my office, as are the children of most of my
friends.

In the same way a classroom or bedroom colorfully
and warmly decorated, but not cluttered, with objects of
interest, will make a child more comfortable. Too much
clutter can be distracting and a hyperactive child could
find it difficult to concentrate. Children with severe
learning disabilities are often, in school, put into plain
cubicles to study, for these children are so easily dis-
tracted that even minimal outside stimuli are destructive to the learning process.

Not only the room environment but even the clothes
an adult wears have an effect on children. One little girl
I know responds very warmly to lace or frills or jewelry.
Most children like a woman to have a soft hairstyle
rather than a severe one. Casual clothes, rather than
very formal or stiff attire, seem to inspire a greater ease
in relating, especially with teenagers. They respond to
clothes that are in current fashion. Teenagers also respond to color. How one dresses is a comparatively
minor issue in relating to a child, but it is nevertheless
one aspect of at least some importance.

Touch Is Often Effective in Communication

More specifically, touch is perhaps one of the most important facets of nonverbal communication with children. Yet it is a tool that must be used carefully, for while most children need it, some are not ready to accept it. Adult intuition plays an important role here. You have to feel when a child needs and is ready for touch.

Children who have no severe emotional problems usually respond positively to a hug or a pat or to being held while a story is told or a direction is given. But children who have experienced a severe emotional trauma either avoid touch entirely or they respond almost exclusively to being held and touched. One little girl came in to see me after the sudden death of her father. She literally flew into my arms and sobbed for the entire hour while I held her and occasionally said something. During the last five minutes of the hour her sobbing subsided and a very teary-eyed, tired but calm little girl walked out of my office to meet her mother. In this incident, to have done anything but hold her, to have tried to distract her attention with toys, would have been to fail to meet her deepest need head-on. Holding her meant that I accepted her feelings of grief and loss, that I understood her need to cry and to feel close to someone, and that I cared. In this case her mother was too involved in her own grief to even realize the extent of the child's. Furthermore the child's grief just reinforced the mother's pain.

Children don't always understand the words we use to explain life to them, but they understand the warmth of touch. Also, children are often unable to express the feelings that are troubling them and therefore need comfort from nonverbal sources. A four-year-old was taken to see an elderly aunt in a convalescent home before he was brought to school. He was quiet on the way back, but as he was left at the classroom he began to cry. When his teacher asked him what was wrong, Joey replied, "I don't know, I just feel sad." Yet after being held for a while and being told he was cared about, Joey calmed down and joined his class. Verbally, his feelings were only vaguely expressed, but the caring that a busy public school teacher showed through touch, solved the problem without many words.

Adults, however, often feel vulnerable to touch. They find it easier to express themselves with word or action, such as helping a child find a book or play with a toy. Just as a child should never be forced to be held, so an adult should not push himself beyond that which feels comfortable to him. If he does, the awkwardness of his feelings is liable to be felt by the child who may interpret it as a form of rejection. Adults, like children, can learn to accept and give touch, but the process is gradual and comes partially through increased positive experience. Try a pat on the shoulder before a hug. Or, with a smaller child who resists touch, a hug before actually picking him up. When a child or an adult stiffens at the feeling of physical contact with another human being it is a signal to go slowly.

During adolescent years problems of touch become sensitive and awkward at times. In our culture, boys feel too grown up to handle much physical contact from a parent. Yet some contact is often secretly desired as well as appropriate. A mother is wise to kiss her son on the cheek rather than the mouth—but *never* in the presence of his friends. Fathers too should try not to feel awkward in extending a pat or a hug to their sons, but again perhaps in privacy.

For a father, the teenage daughter often presents the greatest dilemma. A cuddly little girl suddenly becomes a woman with breasts and menstrual periods. When this happens many men fear sexual attraction to their own daughters. But at the same time their daughters may be overly conscious of the physical changes occurring in their bodies. Yet girls at this age need physical affection from their fathers. Thus when a girl is experiencing over-sensitivity about the development of her breasts, for example, a tactful father will avoid touching her in that area by hugging her sideways or by squeezing her arm. The temporary sensitivity will pass but the father-daughter relationship will perhaps be a little stronger as a result.

Facial Expressions Communicate to Children

If you tell a child that you are not angry at him, and you say it with a scowl, he will believe the scowl, not the words. If you smile warmly at your child's new friend he will feel you like him even though you haven't said so.

A teenager was told by his mother that his parents were well able to help him through medical school and to pay for his counseling with me. Yet he came to me in a state of panic, feeling that his parents' financial resources would never hold out. When I asked him why he thought this after he had just been told that his parents had the money, he replied, "My mother kept avoiding my eyes, like little kids do when they lie, and her jaw was tight and firm as though she was trying too hard to convince me."

With small children, something as seemingly trivial as

direct eye contact is important. To look down from adult height at a child and attempt to communicate is to put yourself at a great disadvantage. Stooping down to his level and getting direct eye contact is much more effective. The child will be able to better concentrate on what you are saying and he will not feel overpowered by your physical size and strength.

Tone of Voice Is a Communicator

Coupled with the importance of facial expression in communicating with children are certain tones of voice.

On several occasions I have had a child come to my office and say, "I don't like school because my teacher screams." When I really check the story out I find that the teacher doesn't say anything upsetting at all. It is simply the tone of voice. One child refused to go to school for that reason.

Certainly the tone of voice we use in expressing our thoughts to someone is important all through our lives. How often I have heard a husband or wife say of their mate, "He says he loves me but the words sound meaningless and flat." And to very little children, where words are not always completely understandable, the inflection of the voice and the look on the face are of paramount importance.

Not long ago a husband and wife sat in my office actually communicating for the first time in many weeks. Sue held her three-week-old baby in her lap who, at first, seemed relaxed and contented. As the couple's voices became louder and louder I watched a calm baby become almost hysterical in his crying. Sue tried to feed him but still he sobbed until I suggested that she let my secretary hold the child for the remainder of the session.

Three-week-old Eric did not understand the words that were said. If he had they would have encouraged him. But he did react violently to angry, loud voices.

Nervous Habits Communicate

Clenching hands, twisting rings and strands of hair, picking at buttons, doodling, pulling at neck chains all indicate unspoken emotions ranging from anger to boredom. I recently watched a well-known celebrity on a TV talk show whose face was completely placid but who, for about the first ten minutes of the show, grasped her hands and shifted her body position as though she was suffering from great nervousness, as perhaps she was. Yet from her speech one would never have observed that tension. In such small ways children too pick up our feelings toward them. Focusing your eyes on the one speaking to you says: "I'm listening, I am interested"; while looking around a room while anyone at any age is talking can be a good indication of disinterest or at least a lack of understanding.

Silence Is a Form of Communication

Another important means of nonverbal communication is silence itself. When a five-year-old asks me for the fifth time if we can go to the toy store, silence and perhaps the expression on my face tend to finally terminate the argument more effectively than further words. The silence that accompanies touch, when words seem trivial or lacking, can express deep understanding and caring. By silence a person can express deep anger, deep love, rejection, acceptance and a number of other feelings.

Because silence can express so many different things,

the adult should be careful that he is accurately conveying the feelings he wants to convey. He can sometimes do this by the use of a few words at the right time. For example, a mother who was furious at a friend came home seething with anger, but silent. However, she immediately broke that silence temporarily to tell her ten-year-old, "I'm very angry, but not at you. You have nothing to do with this."

Acts of Love Are Great Communicators

A great many small, nonverbal acts of love can be exchanged between a child and an adult. When I was a child, rainy days meant home-baked desserts or some kind of special dinner. My best memory of walking into the house after school was the delicious aroma of good food—an aroma which in a subtle way spoke of love.

When one of my patients knows she will arrive home from shopping after her thirteen-year-old daughter gets home from school, she leaves a plate of cookies or a special after-school treat of some kind by the note telling her when she'll be back. Another mother puts a rose in a vase by her daughter's bed after she's finished her morning cleaning.

Children too express love in small, subtle ways. A little girl who crosses a vacant field on the way home from school brings her mother a bouquet of wild flowers. A crumpled-up crayoned picture, a badly made cold cup of instant coffee, and even a treasured frog that scares a parent out of his mind all show love.

Several times I have worked with children who spoke little or no English. There, perhaps more than anywhere else, the importance of nonverbal communication became apparent. It was amazing how a smile, a gesture, a pat on the arm or holding the hand could all go into making a really warm relationship with someone with whom I had almost no verbal contact.

As a child grows older, words take on greater significance. Yet, at their best, words can only partially express how we feel. And for a child who has just learned to speak, words may be woefully inadequate. Perhaps for these reasons people seem to be increasingly more aware of all the nonverbal aspects of real communication. For love can be seen in a smile and felt in the touch of a hand. And well-concealed anger can be perceived in the brittleness of a voice and the setness of a jaw. It remains for us adults to develop ways of expressing what we really feel. And to do so we must not stop after we have found the right words, for words are only the beginning of our communication.

In Summary

1. A colorful, warmly decorated bedroom—without clutter—will convey to your child that you feel he is important.

2. Children respond to touch. Being held, patted or hugged is a very important facet of nonverbal communication.

3. Both tone of voice and facial expressions communicate to your child what you really mean, regardless of what you are saying.

4. Direct eye contact at his level is very effective when you want your child to concentrate on what you are saying.

5. Nervous habits and silence are also nonverbal communicators.

5
CREATIVE PLAY

"Good-bye, second Mother," Amy murmured softly as she left my office following our final counseling session. Then opening the door again, "I will see you again, sometime, won't I?"

I would miss Amy, for her problems had been tough and deep-seated and we had been close. But she was now recovered and had become a fairly well-adjusted child.

Her mother brought her to me when Amy was eight years old. Single and in her mid-twenties, Amy's mother hardly knew what to do when her daughter ran in front of an oncoming car one day screaming, "I want to die, please let me die!" While Amy had never known her real father her experience with men by the time she was eight was extensive. When her mother and her mother's boyfriends were drunk, Amy had often been sexually molested.

Amy's first session with me was a cautious one. There was a danger in confronting her with what I knew, for she thought the adult world was unaware of her experience of molestation. Unknowing as she was about sex on any sophisticated level, she had an intuitive knowledge that what happened to her was not usual or acceptable. As a result, from dealing with Amy's extreme problems I learned at its optimum the value of using toys and games as a way of learning much about children as well as relating deeply to them. More than that, the technique is not limited to a therapist's playroom but can be dramatically used by many parents in growing closer to their children and ultimately in developing their child's feelings of positive self worth.

With Amy the key to our relationship revolved around little miniature dolls, some cars, and a toy village. She couldn't tell me she had been raped, but she could put the dolls through the trauma that she herself had been exposed to so often. Lady dolls huddled in cars and tried to leave town with gentlemen dolls racing after them. "Will the ladies be caught?" I would ask. "Oh yes," Amy would reply as she increased the speed of the escaping cars. And caught they were and attacked amidst shouts and protestations.

Then suddenly breaking away from the imaginary world she had created she would ask, "Sex is always bad, isn't it?" And as one would explain to a much older child I would try to show her the positive, right side of sexuality. Contented for the moment, she would then often turn to a specific male doll, throw him in prison and slam the tiny door. Standing up she would kick the prison and shout, "You bad man!"

"What did he do?" I would ask. Instantly but briefly

she would usually say, "He hurts children." Then frequently she would have a grandmother-type doll walk by the prison window who would solemnly say, "I brought you up to be better than this."

With some additional dialogue between us, interspersed with the more dramatic play with the dolls, such sessions were fairly typical. Sometimes she wanted me to hold her. At other hours she liked to be told stories or walk down the street for an ice-cream cone while she chatted about school—which she found frightening. But for the most part Amy liked to act out sexual and angry acts with the play dolls. And I watched, listened and occasionally interacted. It was her safe way of revealing herself to me through the shield of dolls, who would not condemn her. Through them she gradually perceived that I did not condemn her either and that she was a lovable, good person with worth.

After a while our sessions dealt more directly with her life now. She told me about her cat who slept with her and asked me how she could stop other children from teasing her for being shy. Sex still bothered her, but now she could talk about it directly. The birth of a baby and the prospect of ever having one frightened her until I explained the process of dilation to her. Then she sighed a deep sigh of relief and enthusiastically demanded, "Let's play pool." And we did.

Amy recovered and didn't want to die anymore. But her recovery was partly due to the safe relationship that we formed through the use of toys. Toys that were safe, a playroom where she was free from censure, and an adult who cared enough to listen and accept her, all combined together to save a child who might otherwise have been destroyed.

Games and Toys Are Vehicles of Communication

Most children are not as severely damaged as Amy. But all children need safe, close relationships with their parents and other responsible adults if they are to grow up as whole people who are comfortable with themselves. The parent who takes the time to sit down on the floor and play with games and toys while he listens to his child's conversation, will learn much about that child. Furthermore, he will say in essence: "You are very worthwhile because you are worth my time and interest."

A parent who gives himself, not just his money or his time at dutiful car-pooling, imparts to a child the valuable feeling of being okay. We live in an age of depersonalization where TV becomes an easy but passive baby-sitter, and caring parents, who really want to help their children, rush dutifully from scout meeting to tap dancing lessons, in essence turning themselves into a shuttle-bus service. Therefore, parents need to see the value of spending creative time with their children, using toys that often cost little or nothing as therapy. Such an investment is priceless.

For the small child the games and toys make communication more spontaneous and free; for, after all, children are vulnerable to the adult world that controls them. A seven-year-old boy felt safe using a green frog hand puppet to say, from a frog's point of view of course, "I hate my teacher." But without the protection of the frog the child might not have revealed his real feelings about his first days at school.

Creative toys like clay, puppets, and even blank paper with crayons can be valuable tools in relating to a child, particularly a child who is shy or afraid of punishment.

Such a child will find himself able to express his feelings safely through toys, like puppets, dolls and drawing, for he doesn't realize how greatly he is exposing himself. In turn the parent should be careful to keep his secret and not let him know the extent of his exposure.

One quiet little girl who had been abandoned by her parents showed her anger to me by drawing every person in heavy red and then gleefully exclaiming, "He's bleeding badly!" Once she finished, her anger seemed released for the moment and she was her usual warm, cuddly self. She felt safe and good because she hadn't said anything directly but had expressed her negative feelings. And we were a little closer for the experience.

A child's level of self-esteem is often graphically displayed as well as elevated through toys. An eleven-year-old boy fought to build a complicated model airplane while his father looked on. Finally, throwing the plane down, Jim exclaimed, "I can't do it, I can't do anything right." His father wisely talked to the boy for a while and asked him what things were hardest for him. Because the father came through accepting and warm in both his words and his tone of voice, Jim dared to trust him. He explained his difficulty in throwing a ball in baseball and his utter feelings of failure in math. The result was some hours of help in both areas from his father and a greatly improved father-son relationship. Moreover, because his father understood him, knew his weaknesses and still loved him, Jim grew to like himself better. An eleven-year-old boy, who had extensive heart surgery, felt different from other children his age, and thus inadequate. He loved to have his older sister play GI Joe with him. In his fantasy he, together with the noted army hero, achieved great feats of valor and was decorated with countless medals. His sister at times a little bored with the whole thing nevertheless listened, joined in and made her brother feel the worth that is felt when one is understood and loved.

Parents can observe and foster a multitude of other qualities through the use of toys. One thrifty mother used to take her four small boys to the grocery store and gather up empty cardboard boxes. Once home the boxes became forts, battlegrounds, Indian villages and other imaginary places. Their mother went about her work while the children created their own worlds. Later, however, she commented on how much she learned about her boys from those boxes. The two middle boys always gave in; the youngest wanted to dominate. Some were more sensitive; each had a varying attention span.

The use of simple objects like boxes, where the creative applications are endless, is particularly good in stimulating spontaneity in children. They are also valuable to hyperactive children who have a short attention span. These children can change from building houses to building cities and on to other imaginary games without losing interest. In contrast, the hyperactive child might well become bored and restless with a more structured form of play after just a few minutes.

Creative Play Helps Establish Sexual Identity

One other vital area that a parent can affect through creative play is the development of a good sexual identity. Most parents do not realize that a child's sexual image is developing at a very early age and that before age six that identity may be fairly well set. Little girls develop a female self-image basically from their mothers and their ability to relate to men from their fathers. With boys the reverse is true. Their male identity comes largely through their relationship with their fathers and their ability to relate to women from their mothers. Fortunately other significant adults also influence this sexual role development. A kindly uncle or close aunt may positively influence a child's acceptance of his or her sexuality. The media, children's books, and even advertising also tend to guide a child into the sexual identity which will produce an adult who is heterosexual and thus accepting of his maleness or femaleness.

A mother who takes time to give her little girl clothes to dress up in and the father who shares his sports interest with his son by taking him to ball games will relate positively as female-male figures whom the child will want to emulate. On the other hand, the three-year-old boy who sees nothing but abuse from his father toward his mother or even the child who is neglected totally by his father may have difficulty wanting to be a man.

Most normal children like toys that, traditionally, do not match their sex—boys will want dolls or girls will play with trucks. But real sexual problems can be detected in a child's behavior and play as early as age two. If a parent suspects that his child may have difficulty with his sexual identity he should seek a professional opinion which may, after all, merely end up reassuring him of his child's normalcy. Above all, no child can be *forced* into a masculine or feminine role. A father can't "toughen up" his son by becoming hard and brutal, for example. If there is an abnormal tendency starting, young children respond quickly and positively to good psychotherapy.

The three-year-old boy who cringes from his father's touch and refuses to sleep in anything but frilly pajamas may be headed for trouble. The seven-year-old girl who said to me, "I don't think I have any problems but I do want to be a boy and that's a problem, isn't it?" was having a genuine problem accepting herself as female. Both of these children showed their sexual preferences consistently in their play and were helped by toys. The specific toy used here is not always of utmost significance. What is important is that through the use of a toy which a child can enjoy the child develops a trust and a feeling of positiveness toward the adult involved in the play.

JoAnn, the seven-year-old, always chose to be a boy in a game we played call Life. In the office with me and at home with her mother, who was very intelligent and cooperative, playing Life was helpful, not only because we could watch JoAnn's choices but we could talk about them.

"Why do you want to be a boy?" her mother once asked. "Because if you're a girl you can't defend yourself," answered JoAnn.

Her mother explained in detail that girls could often stand up for themselves and still be feminine and they discussed the topic. More important, JoAnn developed, partly through games, a positive relationship with me and her mother in place of the earlier negative one. Seeing us as women whom she respected and liked made her want to be a woman. The result of such incidents now, a few years later, is a happy teenager who enjoys being a girl.

Disturbed children are greatly helped by therapy that involves the use of games and toys. But equally important, vast numbers of very normal children who, even at young ages, show problems common to the majority of the human race can benefit from a parent relationship which can be developed through toys.

Games Foster Preteen Communication

Not only small children benefit from creative play. While small children are sometimes more fearful in direct conversation and operate more honestly in an aura of imagination and fantasy, preteens are at the awkward, secretive age when communication is often terribly difficult. So many parents of seventh-grade children seek help for a child who is really not all that disturbed. He just isn't the sweet cooperative person he was as a small child.

For preteens who don't yet easily converse with adults in adult fashion, games again can be a useful tool. With my patients of this age group I simply inform them that if they feel reluctant to talk that's fine, but perhaps we could play a game of pool or some other game like Score Four or checkers. The purpose here, in even greater contrast to playing with small children, is more to loosen up the young person so that almost unconsciously he begins to talk, rather than to gain insight.

It's very easy, for example, while you're aiming at a pool ball to ask how school is. When a young person beats you at a dart game or makes a sharp move at checkers there is a perfect opportunity to compliment his or her skill. And one good thing about most of these games is that they can be played without much concentration, leaving time for conversation.

Once again it is the time given that means much to a parent-preteen relationship. I have had children in this age group ask me how *they* can relate better to their parents, while the parents weren't even aware that the need existed. Nor was this always the parents' fault, for children at this age can be dreadfully noncommunicative and even rejecting when underneath they have a deep desire to be close to their parents.

Games with the preadolescent function for the most part as a catalyst which precipitates involvement and communication. One young boy who had been having some minor school problems came to see me and, typically, acted fidgety and reluctant to talk. And nothing turns a child off faster than inviting him to sit in a black leather chair with the implication: "TALK!"

After informing me of his resentment about being in my office, Marc settled down long enough to hear me say: "Try coming here for just a few times and after that if you still want to quit I'll help you convince your parents that you should be allowed to make that decision."

Experiencing a degree of contentment, Marc began to relax. His glance wandered from me to the room we were in and he saw the pool table. "Can we play that?" he asked as he wandered over to the table and picked up a ball, throwing it slowly up into the air.

After several games of pool Marc began to ask me questions. Why was I a therapist? What kind of people came to see me? Did needing help mean a person was crazy? Then, almost forgetting himself and his resolve *not* to become involved, Marc slumped into the nearest chair and began to talk earnestly about the failure and frustration he felt at school.

Such a pattern is typical with the preteen. A parent will converse more meaningfully with his or her twelve-year-old child while they are engaged in almost any activity than if the child is commanded to talk. Even household tasks like peeling potatoes, cleaning the garage, pulling weeds or setting the table are casual enough scenes where the young person just may forget himself and express some real feelings. Relating with your child at this age is on a more feeling level than is communicating with younger children through toys. It involves helping a child to forget himself and to develop a deep gut level trust in the adult involved—an adult who obviously cares enough to spend time with him, yet who respects him enough not to push and loves him enough to listen when he does feel like talking.

Sometimes when you've tried everything and think you've failed, you haven't; for, once again, this age is very secretive. Games help them talk but it takes time and patience on the part of the adult. A young hyperactive, sometimes belligerent girl whom I sometimes think I reach but often feel only frustration over, surprised me the other day and confirmed to me that playing, talking and in general "hanging in there" with children this age does work. I saw Marcia for the first time after the death of a very dear uncle of mine. Marcia and I went out to get a Coke that day while we talked. At the end of the hour as she was leaving, Marcia turned to me and said shyly: "I'm sorry about your uncle—I love you." Then abruptly she took off down the stairs, for the moment overwhelmed by her openness.

Perhaps one of the greatest differences between relating to small children and those a little older is that small children often don't really know or understand their feelings. Additionally they are often overwhelmed by the adult world. Thus toys are tools to bring out their thoughts more clearly and more safely. Preteens, on the other hand, feel silly talking about their emotions and

71

are terribly sensitive about what people will think when they do talk. Besides, they feel grown up enough to have secrets and young enough to need to confide all. They are in between, neither child nor adult, and so they often feel misunderstood by both age groups.

What Kind of Toys and Games?

In the middle of life's problems, at any age, relationships help because they give us confidence and make us feel loved. Toys can help in the development of such a relationship between a parent and a child. At this point, however, the average parent may well ask, "What toys?" or "How can they be used?" Or, more generally, "This all sounds great for a trained child therapist, but how can *I* do this with *my* child?"

Toys that parents can use range from the free, creative types like clay or hand puppets to the more structured games like Life or Aggravation. Creative toys are particularly valuable in drawing children's feelings out into the open. As he draws a picture, for example, a child can be asked to explain his drawing by a simple statement like, "Tell me about it." Most children who play with Fisher-Price dolls or the Fisher-Price village begin to automatically tell stories about the dolls. The child feels free and safe, and may often show feelings that range from aggressiveness—having all the dolls fight or drowning them—to feelings of warmth as he tucks all the dolls into bed in a playhouse or play camper.

But whatever the choice of toys, a parent should do what feels comfortable to himself as well as the child or the effect will be phony. Sometimes, for example, a parent can take two hand puppets, male and female, ask the child which he wants and then let the child choose what roles they'll play. Sometimes the child will say, "I'll be the teacher, you be the student." Or, he may choose to be a parent while the parent plays the child. Don't become too analytical about what he says, for his remarks about parents or teachers may well reflect a friend's feeling rather than his own. Yet certain remarks may give clues to his own real feelings. Totally negative statements about school, for example, may require the parent to check further into how well the child is doing in school, socially as well as academically.

For the parent who feels strange talking through the blank face of a hand puppet, games like Life may better serve his purpose. Again he will learn much about his child. One child stopped suddenly in the middle of Life and asked, "Can I cheat, just once?" When her mother wisely asked "Why?" instead of angrily saying no, the child replied, "Because I'd like to give you an extra turn since you're so far behind." There was a brief but eternal feeling of warmth between the two. Far more important than insight are the tremendous feelings of closeness that come when children and parents relate in that magical world where children live when their imagination and creativity are encouraged.

Timing is a vital facet of creative play. Play shouldn't be forced or done when either the child or parent is too overtired to enjoy the experience. Sometimes people simply don't feel like crawling around on the floor putting together Lego blocks or matching wits with an eight-year-old in a prolonged game of Monopoly. Again, spontaneity is best. Some evenings it just could be a relief to pretend you're a green frog talking to your four-year-old son rather than to think about the day's business deal that went sour. And at times your daughter's dollhouse and her imaginary stories about the people who live there might be more interesting than your recent argument with your in-laws.

Commerical toys, homemade games, and anything that safely brings out a child's feelings and helps develop a relationship between parent and child, should be used by parents with their own children. It is true that the parent will not have the developed skill of a therapist in knowing how to use these tools, nor will he always have the same objectivity, for it is his child. But who can influence a child more than the parent who lives with him every day of the week? To that degree, in the non-technical use of the term, every parent becomes his own child's therapist in all the little and big problems that arise whether he chooses that role or not. Learning to use toys effectively can perhaps help many parents to more positively influence their child as he develops into a person of value to himself and to others.

The world of a child is different than the world of an adult. That is one reason why the fantasy of toys and games works in trying to reach out to their world. In a way the simple description of a child's thought toward his teacher in the book, *The Geranium on the Window-sill Just Died but Teacher Went Right On*, expresses his world accurately:

> Teacher, let me swim in a puddle,
> let me race a cloud in the sky,
> let me build a house without walls.
> But most of all,
> let me laugh at nothing things.

And in contrast the child's attitude toward much of the adult world is echoed in that same book in the following words:

It's September again
—hiding behind my reading book
breathing quietly,
afraid![1]

In Summary

1. A parent can learn much about his child when he sits down on the floor and plays with games and toys while he listens to his child's conversation.

2. Parents help their children establish sexual identity by engaging in creative play to model positive female-male figures.

3. A parent will converse more meaningfully with his preteen while they are engaged in almost any pastime—games, activities, chores.

4. The toys parents can use to communicate with their children range from creative types to structured games.

Notes

1. Albert Cullum, *The Geranium on the Windowsill Just Died but Teacher Went Right On* (copyright by Harlin Quist, 1971), p. 7.

6
SPECIAL THINGS WITH CHILDREN

It was a bright, brisk autumn day when I, an eight-year-old child, stood at the end of the Malibu pier with my father and cut up my own bait for fishing. My sister was fifteen, bored with the scene, and away for the day. But for my father and me the sea, the salt breeze blowing on our faces, the smell of fish and the adventure of fishing were all our thing together. And now, as an adult, I still seek out the sea for comfort and strength. However, it is my thing alone or with a friend because my father is not here.

As a little girl it was a time of one-to-one aloneness with my father. I learned that he and his father built a boat in Chicago and that my father was actually born on a ship in the Stockholm harbor. He learned that I could put bait on a hook and really catch a fish even though I was a girl. We became closer in our sharing and liked each other better. Today I am back at the Malibu pier, an adult, not fishing, just walking and I realize the impact on my life of those times alone with my father.

One-to-One Closeness Is a Special Time

In a similar way many parents could help their children by giving them a time all their own each day. Perhaps a few minutes before bedtime when the child could express his feelings and ask his questions—and when he could count on that time regularly. Time alone in a restaurant, a walk by the beach, a game of checkers or just throwing a ball—these all can be times of sharing and growth between a child and his parent. These are times of special one-to-one closeness. And once again they make a child feel unique. Anything *special* does that for all of us—whether it is a special time or special thing.

These are the many small but important ways parents can help their children grow up feeling good about themselves. Meals, particularly in the evening, can be a tremendous time for forming relationships with children. The ideas available are as creative and numerous as the parents who invent them. One mother I know allows each child to completely plan his or her birthday dinner. No adult authority is imposed—even if the adults who are invited gag over the choice of food. Relatives who are invited are warned that the meal may not be particularly nutritious or well-balanced.

On her last birthday, the six-year-old in one family chose: chocolate milk, chocolate cake, chocolate ice cream, potato chips, spaghetti, and finally, with a little suggestion from her mother, a nutritious salad. The dinner was served very specially in the dining room with the family's best crystal, china and silver. Nancy felt like a princess. It was truly her day and her birthday dinner. She was very special. And in reality the dinner was no worse than the junk kids eat at Halloween, Christmas or Easter.

Every family seems to groan when leftovers are used. Yet in one family they are part of a very pleasurable event. They are not called leftovers—they are called smorgasbord. Dinner is served smorgasbord-style but it is eaten by candlelight, and so the setting implies a special occasion. Leftovers are taken out of the refrigerator and heated—maybe a piece of chicken, part of a pot roast or a serving from a casserole. The mother usually makes a fresh extra dish like a nice salad. Then each member of the family chooses his own separate meal. Being able to choose his own thing—be it clothes, food, or other things—helps in a child's growth as an individual and deepens the relationship between him and the adult who trusts these choices to him. Furthermore, during this meal the parents eat more leisurely and make a point of conversing with the children. So again, the children feel special.

Once again there are times when it may be helpful for a child to eat alone with one parent. A nine-year-old boy who had a special dinner meeting of cub scouts felt especially proud because it was an occasion to which he could bring his father. As he dressed carefully in his scout uniform, his five-year-old sister was putting on her favorite dress and feeling equally proud. Rather than sitting at home feeling jealous of her husband's night out with their son, mother decided to take her daughter, who envied her brother, out to dinner with her. Afterwards it was hard to tell who of the four enjoyed the evening the most. And it was a beautiful way to avoid a left-out feeling in any of them. It is true, in some situations that arise from time to time in our lives, we are all left out. But feeling "left out" can be avoided.

Taking children to a fancy restaurant rather than always to a cheap hamburger drive-in makes them feel important and trusted. I have happy memories, as a small child, of going shopping with my mother and then going to a tearoom for lunch. I felt very grown-up ordering what I wanted and having people comment on how well I behaved. I was expected to behave well and so I did. And I learned to appreciate atmosphere—tastefully served meals, attractive chandeliers, and all that goes with a nice restaurant. So, apart from feeling special, there were other good benefits from the experience, too. We were not rich, but my parents thought that these times were important—and they were.

Exclusive Belongings Are Special

Another way in which a child may feel unique is in the parts of his world that belong to him exclusively. If he shares a bedroom, he can still have his own toy chest or chest of drawers for his clothes. Each child should also have some choice in the clothes he wears, and they should be his alone. I like to see children own books and learn to cherish them as friends that can be read and reread. Even a toy should belong to one child, unless it is a more expensive one, or large in size like a swing.

But apart from the usual, children need things that are exclusively theirs other than clothing or a bedroom. For some it may come in the ownership of a pet or even a plant. One little girl I know hated tomatoes. Yet now that she owns her own tomato plants, she relishes eating each one as it ripens. A woman who is unusually creative with her children made a bulletin board for each of her children's bedrooms. They provide a spot where each child can put what he treasures on display for his world to see. Posted on the five-year-old's bulletin board was something as trivial (to an adult) as the first two phone numbers she had learned to dial by herself. Each board was made personalized. Christy's is very feminine with daisies. Jamie has his name and various athletic symbols on his. In an indirect way a parent's consideration of a child as an individual makes the child feel closer to this person who understands him.

Professional Counseling Is Special

Perhaps counseling involves one of the most unique relationships in the world for it is the closest human relationship in the sense of exposure and, hopefully, trust. It is a safe place, warm and accepting, but honest. It is love without strings and it fosters growth much as a catalyst releases a chemical reaction in a chemistry laboratory.

It was time for Debbie to see me in my office but when she walked in I could see that it was not me alone she needed. On this day Debbie longed to talk to her real mother from whom she had been separated for six months. Debbie's mother had suffered from tuberculosis and had just come home to recover. Debbie had lived for six months in a foster home.

"Would you like to call your mother?" I asked after taking one look at her face. I knew she needed that, yet she would be afraid. For in her five-year-old mind her mother had left and rejected her. She needed the safety of me and my office where our relationship had grown deep. But she needed her mother.

"Hi," she said softly as she heard her mother's voice. "I miss you." Then tears—tears of joy.

"I like the way you cook eggs in the morning," she continued. Then loosened up by trivia, she began to chat. When she left my office that day she was relaxed and seemed happier. Quietly she confided in me that she would tell her foster mother about the call after lunch, obviously afraid that she would hurt her.

For Debbie, on that one day, the privacy of a counselor's office and the warmth of that relationship provided a unique one-to-one special time.

Many times when a child has a problem, a parent or understanding friend may be a great help. Certainly that help should and can continue even if professional counseling is begun. Counseling, however, takes time. It is more than waving a magic wand. TV story-type solutions are not frequent in real life. A problem that takes years to develop will take time to remove. The younger the person, however, the better chance there is for successful counseling for that person.

Whether a child is helped by the parents alone or by a counselor's services, a child's emotional health must be viewed as a very precious thing. A child who is crippled emotionally will grow into an adult who will probably function below his capabilities and will suffer more pain than someone with good emotional health.

I remember one little girl with large blue eyes and beautiful blonde curls—and a very unhappy look on her face. Her parents brought her to me more out of guilt than love. When she cried they spanked her. No one ever held her or told her she was loved except for a grandmother who had recently died. One day she looked sadly out of the window of the playroom and said, "Can't I go where my grandmother is?" Shortly after that her counseling sessions were stopped because no one had time to bring her. How many are there like her, I wonder, who hurt and strive and reach out but whose lives are so deeply damaged and neglected that one can only speculate as to their future.

Fortunately, most parents do care about their children's welfare. For a child brought up in a home where there is love and concern, there is every chance for the development of good emotional health, whether it comes just naturally or whether some problems arise that require some additional help.

Seeking professional help does not mean that you are a total failure as a parent. You may have one child with problems and another one who does not have special problems because the set of circumstances surrounding each of their lives during their formative years was different. Outside factors, like a severe physical illness, may enter into the problem. Above all, parents are human too and sometimes make big mistakes before they are aware of them. It is a stronger parent, however, who can admit to a problem or even a mistake and seek help for it.

A question I am frequently asked is, "How do I tell my son or daughter where he is going?" Again, going for help should not be an issue that is magnified into a put-down. One parent who was counseled herself merely said, "I need someone to talk to about the things that bother me and I want you to have that same chance." The chance for counseling should be presented in a casual way and as an opportunity, something they'll grow to like, not as a punishment.

Many times children, particularly teenagers, come

unwillingly at first. I have no objection to that, although it doesn't make my job easy. However, after a while if a child still resists and learns to actually dislike the counselor, the sessions should probably be terminated with him.

A basic question any parent might ask is, "When does a child need therapy?" A number of questions honestly answered might be of help to such parents.

Does my child seem troubled more often than not?

Is he or she always alone and moody?

Does my child seem to constantly be a problem at home and/or at school?

Am I as a parent basically angry at my child?

Have several people suggested that my child receive professional help?

Is my child too good, too quiet, too adult?

Do his or her problems persist?

The human personality is a fragile thing at best. It takes little to bring a child into this world. But how that personality is developed, whether the child gets the support and help he needs, is a great challenge and becomes, at least for a while, the sacred trust of his parents.

In Summary

1. Each child should be given a time all his own with his parent each day.

2. Each child should have some belonging that is exclusively his, that he doesn't have to share with anyone else.

3. Professional counseling is a special experience.

7
GROWING
THROUGH
PROBLEMS

At 10:00 one Saturday morning Tommy was brought home by the police. He had been turned in by the manager of a local dime store for stealing some caps for his cap gun. It was not the first time he had been caught stealing, but it was the first time the police had been brought in.

Mrs. Stanton was home alone, except for two younger children, Mary, five, and Jimmy, eight. Mr. Stanton was out of town on business and wouldn't be home until Monday. Mrs. Stanton couldn't help but wish that her twelve-year-old son had waited to pull his latest prank until his father was home.

Embarrassed at what the neighbors might think about seeing the police at her house and confused over how to handle the situation, Mrs. Stanton hurriedly said to the officer standing at her door, "Thank you for bringing

Tommy home. I'm sorry you were put to this trouble but I promise we'll get some help for him."

As she closed the door and stood looking at her son she felt very angry. Why was this child hurting all of their lives? Just before her husband left for his trip they had an argument about Tommy. Mr. Stanton felt that they should clamp down on him and "let him know who's boss." His wife felt that he needed professional help, which had been recommended by the school and now the police. It seemed as though all they did these days was fight over Tommy.

Both parents lived in a shadow of fear; fear of what the neighbors would think; fear that their other two children would also develop problems; fear that their own marriage was being permanently affected. Mrs. Stanton found herself picking at everything Mary and Jimmy did. She magnified something like a stolen cookie into a criminal act. And increasingly she was becoming angry at this child who was so oblivious to all of their unhappiness.

Mr. Stanton was reacting in his own way. Rather than becoming critical and sensitive like his wife, he simply avoided much of the unpleasantness. He came home later and later from work and extended his business trips beyond what was necessary. When he was home he avoided as much conflict as possible by absorbing himself in television or even in sleep.

Unfortunately, the Stantons are not unusual. With a different set of circumstances and different people, the same basic problems exist in many homes. For it is impossible for a child in a family to have a problem without that problem affecting every other member in that family. Until that fact becomes apparent in some final action, like a divorce, it is usually hidden, frequently even from close friends.

Problems Can Produce Anger and Guilt

Parents who have a child with a problem will find that they have a fluctuating, confusing reaction toward that child. While they still will love him, they will also frequently feel anger toward him. Such feeling is normal, for in spite of how much the child is hurting, the parent is hurting too, and anger is a normal reaction to pain. If the child's problem is allowed to develop to even greater proportions, the parents' anger will mount also. For example, before she sought help the parent of one preteenage boy actually became afraid that he would physically abuse her. With such feelings of fear, her level of anger was obviously very high. It is better for the child and the parent if a problem is handled before it reaches such intensity.

In some instances anger is increased because the parents feel guilty over the child's problem. At this point the parent attempts to shift guilt. The father who learned of his daughter's stealing problem became irate over the "terrible friends she had" who "made" her become this way. To put the responsibility on his daughter for her own behavior made him feel that he was, in some way, responsible. So by shifting the responsibility from himself to her friends, he freely hated them.

Other parents are more direct. The mother whose little girl was unhappy at school and wouldn't play with other children felt pain over her child's pain—but she also was angry because of the guilt she felt for having, as she put it, "caused that problem."

A correct handling of such guilt feelings will help

reduce the anger that a parent feels toward a disturbed child. It is true that, in varying degrees, parents are the strongest influence in a child's life and therefore are realistically involved in the problems such a child develops. Yet most parents try to do the best they can in raising their children, and since their mistakes are unintentional their level of guilt should not be very high.

In some cases, however, parents may have very little control over the formation of the child's problems. A catastrophic illness in a family may hurt a child, but the parents can hardly control its occurrence. For example, a nine-year-old boy whom I have seen over a period of months was ill during most of his childhood. Emotional scars from that illness remain with members of the family which were beyond the ability of the parents to avoid. In another type of situation involving the same principle, a father tried to raise two small children while he attempted to help an alcoholic wife. They eventually divorced. Now the children have problems but they are not the fault of the father. He did a very good job under unusually bad circumstances.

Whether a parent directly or by circumstance contributes to the development of his child's problems, usually he or she does it without any or much awareness. It is both unfair and unfruitful for a child or the parent himself to lay a heavy load of guilt on the parent. If the parent did the best he knew how, he should not feel guilt. For the child, throwing guilt at his parent is destructive in a variety of ways.

One young boy I knew, who was heavily into the drug scene, went to a psychotherapist. This professional spent the first hour in analysis of the boy's past. After the session he said to the boy, in front of his parents,

"No wonder you're on drugs. You have every reason to be. Your parents are completely to blame, not you." When the boy saw me later he had the perfect cop-out. "My parents made me this way," he said. "No way is anyone going to make me put down drugs. Even my therapist agrees with me." I am sure the therapist did not mean to have this effect on the boy. But he provided the rationale for the boy's continued use of drugs.

Guilty or not, for the parent to go around guilt-ridden, or for a child to wallow in self-pity and anger over what his parents have "done to him," produces no constructive results. The child is only given the added problem of increased anger and/or avoidance in solving his problems. The parent becomes angry and either hates himself or takes it out on his child, spouse, friends—or everyone.

Problem Children Sometimes Produce Overprotective Parents

A less common problem, but one which occurs often enough, is the tendency to overprotect the child who has problems. Sometimes this, too, is done through a sort of misplaced guilt on the parents' part. A mother felt that she didn't take proper care of her child, so he ended up with polio. From then on she wouldn't let him move without her. Ultimately he ended up not only physically crippled, but emotionally disturbed. In some more extreme cases, a parent actually begins to use the child's problems to meet his own neurotic needs. Thus a parent with problems creates problems in the child. In turn that child's problems increase and feed the parent's problems. A vicious, sometimes never-ending cycle is started.

A middle-aged parent brought her very seriously disturbed teenager to see me. As the girl began to show just slight improvement the mother panicked and pulled her out of counseling. She needed her daughter's illness in order to feel needed in a sort of martyr-like fashion. My best guess is that the girl, if she continues without help, will probably end up institutionalized. What a tragic waste of both lives, especially the girl's. But this is one of the more disturbed reactions a parent can have to the emotional problems of a child.

However, not only do the emotional problems of a child affect the parents' relationship with him, they also affect the relationship of the parent with other children in the family. Every parent of a child who uses drugs seems to see that danger in their other children. A thirteen-year-old girl whom I saw for a while had an older brother who was on drugs. The girl was not a doper, but her mother searched her purse and her room, read all her letters and accused her of being loaded every time she was especially tired or excited. She practically pushed the girl into drug usage by her frequent accusations. All this because one child in the family was on drugs.

One family I know raised their two older children with complete freedom and no discipline. As a result the children grew up very insecure and had many problems. Resolved to correct this error, the parents overreacted and were extremely strict with the youngest. The result? He too has many problems because of his parents' attempt to counteract their mistakes with his older brother and sister.

Sometimes other children in a family are neglected because of one child's problems. An eight-year-old who had learning problems at school and was, in general, very hyperactive became the focus of all his parents' attention. Instead of learning from the one child who had problems, they ended up with three children with problems because of their neglect of the children. Nor did their behavior help the first child. Instead, they smothered him and fostered resentment toward him from the other two children.

One family partially solved this problem by having family meetings where everyone's problems were discussed at an appropriate level. Intimate secrets were not revealed; confidences were not broken. But the eight-year-old's fear of school and the twelve-year-old's shyness at school were discussed within the family structure which included two older children. The result was a concerted effort on the part of all to help each other. For example, an older brother met his eight-year-old brother one night a week after school and played ball with him. The younger boy began to associate the school playground with something other than fear and rejection. Furthermore, as other boys joined them he felt a sense of importance and pride over his older brother.

Problems Can Create Family Strain

At times other children become the brunt of a parent's frustration over another child. A parent who may be afraid to show anger toward an already disturbed child may turn it on another child who has done nothing to warrant that anger. I know one mother who put her six-year-old son in a foster home after she had "had it with John," her older son. The six-year-old was bewildered and felt a keen sense of rejection.

More predictable than the effect of one child's problems on his parents' relationship with him and with his brothers and sisters is the fact that in every family where a child has problems there is some strain in the marriage. Perhaps admitting that this is true is a first step toward handling the problem.

In the same way that a parent who devotes all of his time to one child may hurt the other children, so one parent will make his spouse feel neglected. The mother of a girl who was in constant trouble at school and even with the police spent most of her waking hours trying to reason with her daughter and crying over the problem. When her husband wanted to go out for dinner with her alone, she couldn't leave home for fear the daughter would get into further trouble, which she did anyway. When he wanted sex his wife was too strung out or tired. When he wanted to talk about himself, she turned him off either by her disinterest or by turning the conversation back to the problems they had with their daughter. They were Christians who had raised their family in a good church. But because one parent became overly involved in the problems of one child, a once-tolerable marriage was destroyed. After six months of discord and tension the husband began to drink heavily and to seek out women who would listen to him. A few months later he filed for divorce. The wife blames God and wonders why He let this happen, when she is the one who brought on much of the problem.

While most married couples would not go to the extremes mentioned above, there is a tendency to become overly involved with a disturbed child to the extent of harming the marital relationship and also the child. The child not only feels responsible for the discord, but now has the additional concern of his parents' problems.

A bad marital relationship will tend to affect all children involved while a good relationship between a husband and wife is therapeutically good for the children. If there are problems in a home with a child, there is all the more need for parents to have times alone in order to preserve their relationship, which is already undergoing strain.

When there are problems with a child there will be disagreement between the parents on how to handle those problems. Time alone to talk out their differences, as well as to just relax, is vital. One couple I know almost never go to sleep without first talking out their day's activities with each other. After *each* has expressed himself as fully as he needs to, they pray about the things that seem to be problems. No matter how much they may disagree in the heat of the day, this time seems to put them back together. They may not always agree, but they are tolerant of their disagreement and put their relationship above any single disagreement. Such a relationship requires maturity on both sides. It means that a husband emphathizes with a wife who has lived with the family problems all day. It means that a wife understands that her husband cares, but that he too has lived with some problems all day which may be pretty heavy when they are added to the family problems. The husband of a working wife should also realize that she carries a double load since responsibilities for children still probably fall more on her than on him.

A Good Spiritual Relationship Makes Problems Positive

Romans 8:28 reads, "And we know that all that happens to us is working for our good if we love God and are fitting into his plans." For the Christian parent, a right relationship with God will tend to make all the relationships in the family better. A right relationship does not imply a rigid, self-righteous attitude. Rather, a person who has a healthy relationship with God will be more loving, more considerate of people's feelings, more concerned about another's point of view, and less threatened by constructive criticism. That person will not have to force religion on his children or spouse because the reality of that religion will be perceived in many small ways.

Parents who have this kind of spiritual reality will be able to handle the strain that arises from problems within the family with greater ease. Above all, they will find that out of the bleakest problem there will be something "working for [their] good." God does not let His people, who are rightly related to Him, suffer without giving His grace. And one of the greatest sources of suffering for a parent is the problem of his child.

In a somewhat different context, but with similar meaning, Viktor Frankl sums up the meaning of suffering in his book *The Doctor and the Soul.* Frankl knew of suffering in his own unique way. Imprisoned by the Nazis as a young doctor, he lived in concentration camps for three years. Almost all of his family were executed, including his parents and wife. He himself was subjected to a tortured existence in two of the worst concentration camps, Auschwitz and Dachau. After all of that, and perhaps because of it, Frankl wrote: "To subtract trouble, death, fate, and suffering from life would mean stripping life of its form and shape. Only under the hammer blows of fate, in the white heat of suffering, does life gain shape and form."[1]

To "gain shape and form," "to work together for our good," this is the possible outcome of handling problems in as responsible a way as possible. Perhaps the greatest tragedy is not suffering itself but the misuse and waste of that suffering.

In Summary

1. When a child develops problems, parents should not take a heavy load of guilt on themselves nor should they let their child put guilt on them.

2. Guilty or not, for a parent to remain guilt-ridden or for a child to wallow in self-pity and anger over what he feels his parents "have done to him" produces no constructive results.

3. Parents of a problem child should avoid becoming overprotective of their child or of other children in the family who they fear will also develop problems.

4. When there are problems with a child, parents need to spend time together talking out how to handle these problems.

5. A right relationship with God tends to make all relationships in the family better.

Note

1. Viktor Frankl, *Doctor and the Soul* (New York: Alfred A. Knopf, Inc., 1965).